Photography for TEENS

Setting Up the Shot

Photography   Volume   1

by Jason Skog

Content Consultant:
Kevin Jeffrey
Professional Photographer

COMPASS POINT BOOKS
a capstone imprint

Compass Point Books
1710 Roe Crest Drive
North Mankato, MN 56003

Editor: Jill Kalz
Designer: Ashlee Suker
Media Researcher: Svetlana Zhurkin
Production Specialist: Danielle Ceminsky

Library of Congress Cataloging-in-Publication Data
Cataloging-in-publication information is on file with the Library of Congress.
ISBN 978-0-7565-4489-8 (library binding)
ISBN 978-0-7565-4532-1 (paperback)

Image Credits:
Ashlee Suker, back cover (middle), 7, 10, 21, 39; Capstone Studio: Karon Dubke,
back cover (bottom), 8, 9, 12, 14, 15, 20, 22, 24, 25, 32, 33, 40, 41, 44; Dreamstime:
Nickolay Stanev, 27, Toxawww, cover; iStockphoto: igor Balasanov, 19; Jill Kalz, 31,
35, 43; Shutterstock: aggressor (pencil scribble), throughout, Anan Kaewkhammul,
28, Andrejs Pidjass, 18, Andy Z., 42, Elena Elisseeva, 30, GSPhotography, 16, Iakov
Filimonov, 5, Irina Bort, 38, Jason Stitt, 29, JGW Images, 37, Laurin Rinder, 36,
michaeljung, 4, monalisha (dotted circle), throughout, ntwowe, 1 (middle), 17, Olga
Lyubkina, 34, Ryger (background texture), throughout, Tatjana Brila, 23, val r, 26;
Svetlana Zhurkin, back cover (top), 6, 11, 13

Printed in the United States of America in North Mankato, Minnesota.
042012   006696

Table of Contents

Introduction

For many of us, taking photographs is about getting friends or family to look at the camera, counting 1-2-3, and having them say "cheese!" Click. End of story. Maybe there's an occasional picture of the family dog, a flower, or a breathtaking sunset. But for the most part, we don't put much thought into our photos. And the thing is, you can take amazing shots if you just know how to set them up. If you're interested in going beyond the usual, and getting more out of your camera, this book's a great start. Its tips and tricks will teach you to THINK before you CLICK.

Taking photos of friends is quick and easy with a basic point-and-shoot digital camera.

Composition:
Putting Your Shot Together

Professional-level digital cameras have lenses that can be swapped out for different kinds of shots.

No matter what kind of camera you have, there are basic rules and guidelines to follow before you press the button and take your photo. First you have to decide how to frame your subject. Where do you want that person, flower, or building placed with respect to the background and other objects in the shot? How do you make everything within the frame work together? Here are some ideas.

Framing Techniques

An easy way to set up a photograph is to use the rule of thirds. The rule divides the frame into thirds horizontally and vertically. By placing your subject along one of the lines or at the point where the lines intersect, you'll often create a photograph that grabs people's attention. Artists and photographers alike compose images based on this one simple rule, usually without even thinking about it.

This peacock's eye is placed at an intersection point on the rule of thirds grid.

The golden spiral is another technique to help frame your shot. It works well when you have multiple elements in a single scene. The golden spiral looks like a snail's shell. It's a very balanced, naturally pleasing shape. To use this technique, overlay an imaginary golden spiral on your scene, placing the spiral's start point on your main subject. See if you can make the other elements in the scene fall along the spiral's line.

The golden spiral technique places the main subject (the woman) at the spiral's start point.

Some cameras have an option to place a grid of thirds over the display screen. Normally found under the "display" settings, you can turn the function on or off to help you set up a photograph. Practice with these grid lines for a bit. Get used to seeing scenes in thirds. You might soon find you no longer need the extra help.

STEP 1

Go to a park and pick a subject, such as a merry-go-round, a bike, or your best friend. Center your subject in the middle of the camera frame.

STEP 2

Now imagine a grid overlaying the scene and dividing it into thirds.

STEP 3

Move until your subject sits at a point where the lines come together.

Which image do you find more interesting: centered or not-centered?

STEP 4

Continue playing with the subject's placement, moving it to other intersection points or along a whole line.

Sometimes the perfect frame is staring right back at you. Doorways, windows, and trees can spotlight your subject and provide depth to the shot. Color or lack of color can do the same thing. Imagine, for example, a cardinal sitting in an evergreen tree. The green needles act as a natural frame for your subject, the red bird.

The arched opening of a ruin provides a natural frame for this subject.

Background Matters

Remember that the composition of a photograph includes the entire photograph, not just the subject. Consider what's behind your subject. If the background of your photo is distracting or too busy, change your perspective. Take the picture from another angle. Sometimes moving just a few feet can better highlight your subject and make it pop.

If you can't move, maybe your subject can. Instead of having your friend stand in front of a cluttered shelf with stacks of books and magazines, try moving her to a solid-colored wall or have her sit on a neutral-colored couch.

RULES ARE MADE TO BE BROKEN

The rules of photography are rules, not laws. They can be broken. Think of them as guidelines that will help you take better photos most of the time.

For example, in most cases following the rule of thirds will produce a cool shot. But in some cases, it may make an image less interesting. Playing around with subject placement and various angles can create some fun results, even if they're unconventional.

Consider a scene with a lot of symmetry, perfect balance, or long vertical lines, such as a stand of birch trees. Does it look better or more natural to fill the frame with the trees, rather than using the rule of thirds? Take the picture a number of ways. See which you like better.

When in doubt, take a picture. Don't worry whether it's how you're supposed to take it. With enough practice, the general rules will become second nature, and you'll have a better idea of when you can break them.

Suppose your mom, grandma, and great-grandma get together only once every couple years. It'd be a shame if the only picture you have of them shows a giant fern growing out of Great-Grandma's head. Funny, sure. But still, take a moment to move the plant or move Great-Grandma. You'll be glad you did.

Take time to look for light posts or signs behind people's heads too. A step to one side or the other, and the problem's solved.

Backdrops

One way to keep unwanted elements out of the background of your photographs is to use a backdrop. It provides a clean, simple background for the subject you're shooting. It focuses attention on your subject, not the stuff around it. And you don't have to spend a lot of money or be in a photography studio to use a backdrop. It can be something as simple as a bed sheet, a tarp, or even a large piece of cardboard.

A trick shot makes far and near objects appear the same distance away from the camera.

Bringing the Background into Focus

Backgrounds matter, and sometimes they're even the main focus. For a little fun, have a friend pretend to "hold" the sun or other distant object in the palm of his hand. It's a simple optical illusion, and it might take a few tries, but the results can be pretty entertaining.

SIMPLE SELLS

Let's say you have a piece of jewelry you want to sell online. Try placing it on a piece of white or colored paper or on a solid-colored scrap of fabric and curl up the back edge a bit, like a wave. A simple backdrop makes the jewelry the focus of the image. It lets the details shine through and helps you make a sale—or at least a better photograph.

STEP 1

Have two friends stand far away.

STEP 2

Set an apple or other piece of fruit on a bench or table in front of you.

STEP 3

Carefully line up your friends with the apple so it looks like they're standing on top of it.

STEP 4

Encourage your friends to act goofy. Maybe they're both on one leg, looking off-balance. Maybe they're peering off the edge of the apple. Have fun!

Less Is More

In composing a photograph, try focusing on only the subject and its most interesting and important elements. If you're taking a picture of a cat in a sunny windowsill, for example, you probably don't need to include the fast-food cup beside her (unless the cat is drinking from it). It's distracting, and the viewer will be confused about why you took a picture of a cat and a cup.

Simple surroundings make a subject stand out.

Most of the time, the best photos are simple and basic. They include a single subject or a handful of elements that work together as one. Set up your shot so that it includes only those things that are worth including. In other words, edit out the extras and highlight the highlights.

YOU MUST FOCUS

Know what's a bummer? A blurry photo! Make sure your image is in focus. For cameras with auto focus, that means pressing the shutter-release button halfway down, waiting for the camera to focus, and then pressing the button all the way for a crisp, clear image. Keep your hands as steady as possible. Most point-and-shoot cameras will alert you if they have trouble focusing. In that case you may need to move closer or farther away, or increase the amount of light in the area.

Click Away!

If you're not sure how you want your final image to look, shoot first and ask questions later. In the case of digital cameras, take multiple shots of the same subject and then revisit the images later on a computer. You can crop and zoom in and figure out what moved you to take the photo in the first place.

Maybe you're taking a wide shot of a scene with a lot going on, such as a street fair or carnival. Only later, when flipping through the images on your camera or computer, do you discover the coolest part of the photo was happening in a corner. But if you don't take the picture at all, you won't have anything to work with. So, click away!

Chapter 2

The Right Light

L ight can make or break a photo. Simple as that. Too much light, too little light, or the wrong kind of light can ruin a photograph, or at least keep it from meeting its full potential. Light can come from a variety of sources—the sun, a lamp, a flash, a campfire, or even the candles on a birthday cake. Let's take a look at various ways to add, remove, or tinker with light to find the best way to showcase your subject.

Room Lighting

For inside photography, room lighting is the most common. Room lighting comes from lamps, ceiling fixtures, and other light sources typically found indoors. Be careful with overhead lighting, though. Light that comes from above can often lead

Natural outdoor lighting is often the most flattering.

to harsh, unflattering shadows on people's faces. Instead, try turning on lamps so light hits your subject from the sides. Or move your subject to improve the lighting.

Window light is a great alternative for inside photography. It can create a variety of moods, from sad to joyful, depending on the weather and time of day. And best of all, it's free! But be sure to place your subject off to the side of the window, not in front. A subject standing directly in front of a window will appear dark in a photo.

Window lighting on a rainy day can create a sad or wistful mood.

HOLD OFF ON HEAD-ON

Lighting a person head-on can make her look like she's getting a mug shot for a driver's license. Or a wanted poster. Ack! It can be unflattering and unnatural. Try lighting your subject from a 45-degree angle off to the side. The result is a more pleasing, softer look.

Continuous Light

Studio photographers often rely on large lights that are installed permanently and provide a constant, powerful light source that they can direct and control. You can get a similar effect by using high-wattage utility lights, like those used by painters and mechanics. They're portable and bright. Even taking the shade off an old lamp and using a 100-watt light bulb can do the trick.

Clouds Can Be Fun

As helpful as the sun is as a light source, it can also be a hassle. Sometimes it's simply too bright. Other times it's in the wrong place, such as right behind your subject. On those occasions, photographers welcome an overcast day, where the sky is covered with clouds.

Clouds act as a natural filter, softening the harsh, bright light and eliminating shadows. The result is often a more natural, pleasing image. So don't be scared off or disappointed by a cloudy day. You might wind up with better shots than you'd get on a sunny day.

Clouds soften natural outdoor lighting, reducing glare and reflections.

Using a flash can sometimes create a very stark, unnatural photograph or the dreaded "red eye." Although you can minimize red eye with camera settings or fix it later on your computer, there are ways to use a flash that create more natural images. One is to "bounce" your flash up off the ceiling or over your subjects. Separate flash units often have a swivel head that allows you to point it upward.

For cameras with a built-in flash, bouncing the light is a bit trickier. Try taping a small piece of white tagboard or heavier cardstock beneath the flash and angle it upward. This technique will prevent the flash from shooting straight at your subjects and instead lighting the area above them. Play a bit to see what works best for your camera and your environment.

To Flash or Not to Flash

You've got light, but how do you know if it's too little? Or too much? Too little light will lead to a dark or blurry photo. Too much light can wash out colors, create harsh shadows, and erase a lot of the details in your image.

Many cameras have built-in sensors that measure the amount of light entering the lens. If more light is needed for the shot, the camera will tell you to pop up the flash. A flash is a small, bright

light bulb that flashes just for an instant but long enough to make a scene brighter. Some cameras may trigger the flash automatically. Make sure when you hold your camera that your hand isn't blocking the flash!

You'll usually be able to tell if you have too much light. Colors will look washed out or your subject may be squinting. In that case move your subject, turn off a light, or close a curtain.

Digital camera with a pop-up flash

PLAYING WITH DIRECTION

Almost as important as the kind of light you use is the direction of your light source. A subject lit from the front will look very different when lit from behind, above, or below. Outside, your main light source is the sun. Try taking pictures of the same subject during various times of day. Your neighborhood park will probably look more peaceful in the low-angled soft light at dawn or at sunset than it does at midday with the sun high in the sky.

STEP 1

Have a friend sit in front of a neutral background.

STEP 2

Turn on an overhead fixture and see how the light lands on her face.

Take note of any shadows.

STEP 3

Turn off the overhead light and turn on a table lamp. Place it to the left of your friend. How does the position of the light change the way her face looks?

STEP 4

Move the lamp below your friend's face. How does this position change the mood of the shot? When might you want to use this kind of lighting?

STEP 5

Finally, move the lamp behind your friend. Which light position makes her look most friendly? Most frightening?

HERE COMES THE SUN

Few other light sources can compare to the sun. Strong enough to light up an entire football stadium in the afternoon yet gentle enough to cast a warm glow over a lake at sunset, the sun is one dynamic and versatile light source. But the sun can also be frustrating. Because it's so strong, it can create all sorts of harsh shadows and reflections. It can wash out colors, especially on clear summer days.

What do you do? If you have a camera with interchangeable lenses, try a polarizing filter. Basically, the filter gets rid of reflections and glare, allowing colors to appear rich and deep. Leaves look greener. Clear skies look bluer. Water looks like liquid crystal.

Some of the best times to use the sun are during the "golden hours"—typically the first hour of light in the morning and the last hour of light at night. They're called golden hours because that's often the color of the light during those times. Photos take on a beautiful, golden hue.

Types of Photography

chapter 3

Taking shots of the natural world is called nature or landscape photography.

Rules and tools for framing a picture: check. An understanding of proper lighting: check. But what if you don't even know what to shoot? Each type of photography has its own rewards. If you're a people person, portraits or sports photography might be the way to go. If you love history, focus on buildings, bridges, or other types of architecture. Here are some paths to consider.

Portraits

Formally framed and posed pictures of people are called portraits. Portrait photography is often associated with baby pictures, senior pictures, business profiles, and weddings. Portraits are designed to make a person look his or her best, which is why they require more careful preparation of the person or people being photographed. Hair and makeup are done right. Clothes are more formal, clean, and nicely pressed.

Traditional, studio-shot wedding portraits are carefully posed.

To set up a simple portrait, find a neutral background, such as a solid-colored wall, and have your subject sit or stand in front of it. Use soft light. Try window light. Most portraits include just the head and shoulders, but include the whole body if you'd like.

Portraits showcase people, especially their faces.

BACK OFF, BUDDY

Not everybody likes having his or her picture taken. If your subjects seem uncomfortable, give them some space. Try backing away a few feet and then zooming in closer with your lens. Even a little extra distance can make all the difference.

Landscape and Nature

The great outdoors is one of photography's most amazing studios. Photos taken outside—usually without interference from man-made objects—are called landscape or nature photographs. The combination of the sun, weather, changing seasons, and wildlife can create dramatic images. Outside light is constantly changing too. Waiting for and catching just the right light on a lake or cliff side can be magical.

Here's an idea to get you started: Head to your backyard or a nearby park just after a downpour. Look for raindrops sitting on leaves or pooled inside a bloom. Look for trees reflected in

Flowers, trees, and other types of vegetation are all part of nature photography.

wide puddles. Notice the pattern of dark earthworms against the concrete walkway. If the sun's coming out, look for a rainbow. Consider the rule of thirds and the golden spiral when setting up your shot.

Nature photography often requires great patience to land the perfect shot.

Panorama

A panoramic photograph covers a wide angle. It's usually a series of photos stitched together to capture a much larger image than can be seen through your lens, such as a city skyline or a football stadium.

STEP 1

Find a long subject, such as a row of cars, a bridge, or a tree line. Start at the left end and take a picture.

STEP 2

While keeping the camera level, turn to the right. Move just enough so that you keep a portion of what was in the previous shot. Leave no gaps. Take another picture.

STEP 3

Repeat the process as needed.

STEP 4

Later, with photo-editing software, you can line up the images to create one continuous image.

Carry your camera with you around the house and around the neighborhood. You never know when you'll come across a great photo opportunity. Just having your camera with you forces you to pay closer attention to the kinds of scenes that make good photos.

Still Life

A still life is exactly what it sounds like: still, inanimate object or collection of objects. A glass vase. A peach. A can of spilled crayons or marbles.

Lighting, color, and texture play key roles in a still life.

Choose an object that means a lot to you. Maybe it's a signed baseball or a stuffed animal. Place it on a solid-colored surface in front of a plain background. Then experiment with light and shadow by moving your light source around: right, left, up, and down. How does the direction of the light change the look of the image? Look at the object up close, focusing on one detail. Look at it from a distance. Play a bit. After all, it's an object. It'll sit still for as long as you need.

Even a simple bed can be an appealing still life subject.

Action and Sports Shots

Capturing motion can be one of the most rewarding challenges in photography. When the action is fast, your eyes, hands, and camera have to be fast too. Some point-and-shoot cameras have a built-in "sports" or "action" setting. The camera's able to freeze a moment without blurring it. If your camera doesn't have this feature, follow the action with your camera as best you can. For example, if you're at a track meet, follow the long-distance jumper through your viewfinder while she runs, and click the button when she finally jumps.

Don't forget to watch the sidelines for emotional reactions. Zoom in on a player's face while he's waiting to see if a last-minute half-court shot is made. Sometimes the best images come just before or right after the buzzer sounds.

Sports and action photography requires quick thinking and quick hands.

COLOR VS. BLACK AND WHITE

The world is full of color, and it's tempting to want to capture as much of that color as possible in your photos. But before color photography came along, black and white was the only choice.

Most digital cameras give you the option of taking pictures in black and white. Black and white can lend a historic, timeless, or old-fashioned feel to photographs. It can make a portrait feel more honest and real. The contrast between light and dark in a black-and-white photo gives the photo depth.

Take pictures of your friends and family—both group shots and individual portraits—in black and white. Then take some in color. How do the two sets of photos differ? What images look better in black and white? In color? Notice how black and white often brings out details and textures you might not have noticed in color.

Architecture

Everyone's seen a house. A skyscraper. A church. A barn. But finding new ways to capture common structures like these is the challenge in taking a good architectural photograph.

Historical architecture is reflected in this photo of a modern skyscaper.

Some buildings are so special, historic, or striking that it takes little more than pointing the camera and pressing the button. But if you don't live near the Taj Mahal, you might have to work a little harder. Look high and low, not just at eye level. Play with angles and light. Look at the buildings close up, at their nails, doorknobs, or stained glass.

Colorful shutters, stonework, and other details add interest to a building photo.

Night Photography

Streaking headlights on a busy city street. Friends around a campfire. A lit Christmas tree in a snowy backyard.

Night photography takes viewers into a less-familiar world. But shooting at night can be tricky. It takes practice. In dark conditions, a camera needs more time to let in enough light.

STEP 1

Visit your local library early in the morning and look at it from various angles and distances. Lie on your back and look up. Look for interesting patterns in the brick, stone, or wood.

STEP 2

Revisit the library at noon. Look at it again from the same angles and distances. How do the building's colors and shadows change as the light changes?

STEP 3

Visit the library a third time, in the evening. What sort of feeling do you get by looking at it? How does the feeling differ from the feeling you had in the morning?

STEP 4

Stay until night falls. Which time of day produced the most dramatic image? The least dramatic?

It opens and closes its shutter more slowly. Any movement of the camera during a low-light shot can create that biggest of bummers: BLUR. Some point-and-shoot cameras have a "nighttime" setting that automatically controls the amount of light coming in. But you still need a steady hand. It's usually

Intentional blur, created by moving traffic, adds energy to this nighttime photo.

best to use a tripod or other sturdy surface to keep the camera still during night shots. If your camera has a timer, use it. You'll reduce your chances for blur even more if your finger doesn't even touch the shutter-release button.

Close-ups

Also known as "macro" photography, close-ups are all about revealing the smallest details about your subject. Flowers are a popular pick. So are raindrops and bugs. Most close-ups require a macro lens or a special setting on your camera. The trick to getting a great close-up is crisp focus and a steady hand or a tripod.

Macro photography captures images not easily seen in everyday life.

The next time you're at your favorite fast-food place, play with close-ups. A stack of coins on the table. A french fry. The cherry on top of your sundae. It's a whole new way of seeing the world!

ARE YOU READY?

The key to amazing photographs? It's not about pushing the button, the CLICK. It's about being prepared—knowing ahead of time where to place your subject in a frame and how to find the best light. THINK. No matter what kind of camera you have, you can get great shots by taking the time to set them up right. Be ready for that next birthday party. Field trip. Football game. Thunderstorm. And get out and shoot!

GLOSSARY

composition–the way pieces are put together to form a whole

flash–a bright light bulb that flashes for an instant to better light the subject of a photograph

lens–a piece of curved glass in a camera that can bend light and focus images

panorama–a wide view of an area

perspective–point of view

polarizing–changing light waves to reduce reflections and enrich colors

shutter–the part of a camera that allows light in

symmetry–the state of being perfectly balanced along a center line

tripod–a stand with three legs

versatile–useful in many ways

viewfinder–a small window through which the subject of a photograph can be viewed

FURTHER READING

Gaines, Thom. *Digital Photo Madness: 50 Weird & Wacky Things to Do with Your Digital Camera.* New York: Lark Books, 2006.

Styr, Charlie, with Maria Wakem. *Click: The Ultimate Photography Guide for Generation Now.* New York: Amphoto Books, 2009.

ON THE WEB

Use FactHound to find Internet sites related to this book. All of the sites on FactHound have been researched by our staff.

Here's all you do:

Visit *www.facthound.com*

Type in this code: 9780756544898

ABOUT THE AUTHOR

Jason Skog has written several books for young readers. He is a freelance writer and former newspaper reporter living in Brooklyn, New York, with his wife and two young sons.

SELECT BIBLIOGRAPHY

Ang, Tom. *Digital Photographer's Handbook.* New York: Dorling Kindersley, 2008.

Bishop, Sue. *Color, Light, and Composition: A Photographer's Guide.* East Sussex, England: Photographers' Institute Press, 2010.

Joinson, Simon. *101 Great Things to Do With Your Digital Camera.* Cincinnati: David & Charles Limited, 2006.

King, Julie Adair, and Serge Timacheff. *Digital Photography for Dummies.* Indianapolis: Wiley Pub., Inc., 2008.

Wignall, Jeff. *Focus on Digital Photography Basics.* New York: Lark Books, 2010.

Look for all the books in the Photography for TEENS series:

INDEX